ADORABLE ANIMAL BABIES

BABY ANIMALS IN THE OCEAN

SARAH RIDLEY

PowerKiDS press.

Published in 2026
by The Rosen Publishing Group, Inc.
2544 Clinton Street, Buffalo, NY 14224

First published in Great Britain in 2021
by Wayland

Editor: Nicola Edwards
Designer: Lisa Peacock

Cataloging-in-Publication Data

Names: Ridley, Sarah.
Title: Baby animals in the ocean / Sarah Ridley.
Description: Buffalo, NY : PowerKids Press, 2026. | Series: Adorable animal babies | Includes glossary and index.
Identifiers: ISBN 9781499453553 (pbk.) | ISBN 9781499453560 (library bound) | ISBN 9781499453577 (ebook)
Subjects: LCSH: Marine animals--Infancy--Juvenile literature. | Marine animals--Ecology--Juvenile literature. | Marine ecology--Juvenile literature.
Classification: LCC QL122.2 R535 2026 | DDC 591.77--dc23

Manufactured in the United States of America
CPSIA Compliance Information: Batch #CSPK26. For further information contact Rosen Publishing at 1-800-237-9932.

Picture acknowledgements:
Nature PL: Fred Bavendam 26t, 26b; Suzi Eszterhas/Minden 22t; Mitsuaki Iwago 13; Constantinos Petrinos 5t; Jeff Rotman 16; Tui De Roy 14b; David Shale 8t; Tony Wu 6t, 10, 11. Shutterstock: Aphelleon/Elements furnished by NASA 4t; Apple-of-the-earths 15b, 28bl; Nina B 12b; Randy Beveridge 25b; Willyam Bradberry 3; Chelsea Cameron 27t, 28br; Rich Carey 6b, 28tr; Chase Dekker front cover, 2, 18-19b, 20t, 22b, 23t, 23b, 24b, 28tl, 32; Laura Dinraths 7b; Sheila Fitzgerald 24t; Sahara Frost 29cl; Allan Holland 9b; Image Earth Photography 4b; Andrea Izzotti title page,17b,19t; Kjersti Joergensen 15t; Elise Lefran 29tr; Vincent Legrand 18t; David A Litman 25t; Liquid Productions LLC 29tl; nicehelix 14t; Boris Pamikov 27b; Jack Perks 8b, 9t, 29cr; Janos Rautonen 5b; SergeUWPhoto 7t; Monika Wieland Shields 20b, 21Rattiya Thongdumhyu 5c, 29bl; Vkilikov 17t; Richard Whitcombe 12t.

CONTENTS

Words in **bold** are in the glossary on pages 30-31.

OCEAN BABIES

Water covers 70 percent of our planet, making it look blue from space. Most of that water is in Earth's seas and oceans.

Many millions of animals spend their whole lives in water. This baby whale could live for another 50 years.

A slipper lobster is very different from a whale, but her babies will also spend their lives in the sea. She keeps her **eggs** safe under her tail until they **hatch** about a year later.

Eggs

Crab larva

A lot of ocean animals release their eggs and leave. The eggs hatch into **larvae**. Many are so small that we can only see them if we use a **microscope**.

Other ocean animals have one baby at a time and take great care of them. A manatee stays close to her **calf** for about two years.

FISH FRY

Most fish lay millions of eggs over their lifetime and never meet their babies. A baby fish is called a **fry**.

Every year, snappers gather to breed. The females lay their eggs and the males swim over them, releasing a cloud of **sperm**.

Some of the fry will survive to become adults and lay eggs of their own.

Juvenile snappers

A few kinds of fish look after their eggs.

The male jawfish keeps his eggs warm and safe inside his mouth until they hatch into fry.

Clown fish parents stay close to their red eggs, which are stuck to a rock. The father fish cleans the eggs and stops other animals from eating them.

GLASS EELS AND ELVERS

Like most fish, eels **mate** and lay eggs but we don't know a lot about eel mating. Tiny leaf-shaped larvae hatch from the eggs, laid in the Sargasso Sea. This is in the Atlantic Ocean.

Now the larvae begin an amazing journey. Some drift towards North America and the rest drift to Europe on a journey that takes a year or two. They change into tiny baby eels, called glass eels.

The glass eels return to the rivers where their parents lived. They will cross land if something blocks their way. Their bodies turn brown. Now called elvers, they find a good place in a river to feed and grow.

For the next 12 to 17 years, the elvers continue to grow and change into yellow eels. Lots of them are eaten by otters, birds, fish, and people.

Finally they turn silver, swim down rivers to the Atlantic Ocean and back to the Sargasso Sea. They mate, lay eggs and die.

SEAHORSE FRY

Seahorses are fish. They stay with the same partner for life. Each morning, they meet to swim and dance with each other before returning to their own part of ocean nearby.

When it is time to have babies, the female moves her eggs into a **pouch** on the male's body. The eggs grow and grow.

A few weeks later, the father starts to give birth, sending tiny seahorse fry out into the ocean from his belly pouch.

SEA TURTLE HATCHLINGS

Like most **reptiles**, female sea turtles lay their eggs and leave. But first they swim for hours, or even days, to reach the same beach where they hatched.

This one has just arrived.

Using her flippers, a mother turtle pulls herself up the beach and starts digging a **nest** for her eggs.

Next, the sea turtle lays her soft white eggs in the nest, covers them with sand and returns to the sea.

A few weeks later, tiny turtle **hatchlings** hatch and scramble to the top of the nest.

Now they must run as fast as they can to reach the sea before birds swoop down and eat them.

The tiny turtles swim out to sea. Like most reptile babies, they will never meet their mother.

DOLPHIN CALVES

Dolphins are **mammals**. A calf develops inside its mother's body for ten to 16 months before it is born. The mother and calf will stay together for about three years.

During this time, a calf drinks milk from its mother's body but also learns how to catch fish. It can hold its breath but must come to the surface to breathe.

The calf needs to keep up with its mother. Swimming close to her body helps it move through the water.

Mother and calf chat to each other. *Cli-ick-ick-ick-ick, whistle, squ-eal.* The calls help them stay in touch as they swim around the ocean.

Dolphins live in groups called pods. Calves watch, listen and chat to the dolphins in their pods. These dolphins are catching fish.

Jumping out of the water and playing in the waves is fun and helps calves grow strong and learn how to fit in with other dolphins.

Slowly, the calves learn how to **hunt**, stay safe and find their way around the ocean.

ORCA CALVES

An orca is another sort of dolphin. When it is born it stays close and drinks its mother's milk.

Orcas live in families, often led by the grandmother. She leads them around the ocean and knows where to hunt for food.

This orca calf is copying its mother. The mother will also teach her calf how to hunt. Even when the calf is fully grown, they will always stay close.

SEA OTTER PUPS

When a sea otter **pup** is born, its mother needs to keep it warm. She swims on her back to let her pup sleep on her tummy.

The pup's fur is not waterproof yet so the mother blows air into the fur to fluff it up. This helps the pup stay warm.

The mother leaves her baby while she dives down to find sea urchins, crabs, and other food. She must eat to make milk for her pup to drink.

Squeak, squeak, squeak! The pup cries out for its mother if it gets lost at sea. She uses these cries to find her pup, coos to it and dries it off on her tummy.

When the pup is about a month old, its mother teaches it how to swim. They play together in shallow water.

The mother shows her pup where to find food and how to crack open crabs and **shellfish**.

She teaches the pup how to wrap itself in **kelp** so that it can rest without drifting away.

Mother and cub stay close for about a year. This large pup is almost ready to leave its mother but is still taking rests on its mother's tummy!

OCTOPUS HATCHLINGS

Octopus mothers are amazing. They protect their eggs, clean them and blow air over them as they develop. This octopus has wrapped herself around the eggs she laid inside a cave.

While she guards her eggs, the mother eats nothing. After a few months the tiny hatchlings pop out of the egg cases and swim to the surface to feed. Their mother dies.

The hatchlings grow from tiny octopuses into adults. In a year or two, some of them will lay eggs of their own and the **life cycle** will begin again.

CAN YOU REMEMBER?

Now that you have read about some ocean babies, can you remember their special names?

1.

2.

3.

4.

5.

6.

7.

8.

9.

The answers are on page 31.

GLOSSARY

calf a baby whale or dolphin, and the name for other baby animals

egg a rounded object produced inside the body of a female animal, inside which a young animal develops

fry a baby fish

hatch to come out of an egg

hatchling a baby turtle or octopus, and the name for other baby animals

hunt to go after a wild animal to kill it (for food)

juvenile a young animal that is not yet an adult

kelp large seaweed

larva (plural larvae) the tiny young of crabs, insects and many other animals. It looks very different from its parents

life cycle all the stages that a living thing goes through during its life

mammal a warm-blooded animal with a backbone and hair that gives birth to live young. Young drink milk from their mother.

mate when a male and female animal join together to have babies. A mate is also the name for the partner of an animal.

microscope a device that uses lenses to make very small things appear larger

nest a place built by animals in which they keep their eggs or young safe

pouch a flap of skin inside which some animals carry their eggs or young

pup the name for the young of many types of animal, including sea otters

reptile a cold-blooded animal with a backbone and scaly skin, which lays eggs and breathes air

shellfish a sea animal, usually with a shell, such as a crab, lobster or sea urchin

sperm a cell (a tiny living thing) produced by a male animal, that can combine with a female egg to make young

Answers

1. sea otter pup; 2. juvenile fish (fry); 3. sea turtle hatchlings; 4. octopus hatchling; 5. dolphin calf; 6. orca calf; 7. seahorse fry; 8. elver; 9. crab larva

INDEX